T0370322

Reflections

Joshua Carmichael

authorHOUSE®

AuthorHouse™
1663 Liberty Drive
Bloomington, IN 47403
www.authorhouse.com
Phone: 1-800-839-8640

©2010 Joshua Carmichael. All rights reserved.

No part of this book may be reproduced, stored in a retrieval system, or transmitted by any means without the written permission of the author.

First published by AuthorHouse   9/13/2010

ISBN: 978-1-4520-7376-7 (sc)

Library of Congress Control Number: 2010913716

Printed in the United States of America

This book is printed on acid-free paper.

Because of the dynamic nature of the Internet, any Web addresses or links contained in this book may have changed since publication and may no longer be valid. The views expressed in this work are solely those of the author and do not necessarily reflect the views of the publisher, and the publisher hereby disclaims any responsibility for them.

Ladies and Gentlemen,

Enclosed in this packet are 2 books of 72 poems which I have constructed over
the past three years. Each book deals with a wide variety of current subjects and
contains themes which carry on between the chapters as well as both books.
In short, I hope you enjoy them both and I look forward to seeing you again very soon.

Sincerely, Joshua Carmichael

Reflection 09-10

Chapter One

Reflection

Sometimes I find it hard to speak,
Of things we're not supposed to think,
Born older than we'll ever be,
Bolder than before,

In time I'll find the will to be,
This man that stands in front of me,
Still the image of the boy I see,
In this mirror is here and gone,

So tell me who's this stranger,
Stealing my reflection,
In an opposite direction,
Mocking every move I make,

Someone tell me who's the stranger,
Caught up in my vision,
It was always your decision,
To turn and walk away,

Free Fall

All life is in the fallen leaves,
Carried by the coolest breeze,
Down darkened days and empty streets,
In a dream of waking love,

Jesus sings a song of peace,
Hope in prayer,
It is the least,
The beast and prey both thirst to drink,
A faith that can't be stolen,

With broken teeth by silver tongue,
As heavy as the gold you hold,
Let loose the soul and set it free,
Let loose the soul,
Let loose the soul,

Through autumn winds and summer rains,
Bitter winter cold,
Life springs again,
Bringing balance back to shifting weights,
All fate is to be fallen,

Revenge Song

When the world ends,
All your sins will be forgotten,
And as the world burns,
All your souls will finally be together,
In hell where you belong,
With other pious masqueraders,
To fall it is your fate,
Yes the leaves they will be falling,

To thieve,
Your only virtue,

To shake the foundations of the poor,

More's your only sorrow,
Wrong,
Your only moral,

Lured in by the devil,
Evil is your only lore,

Oh yes indeed,
You best believe,
The leaves they will be falling,

Full Circle

After the fact,
But before the effect,
Comes the transitional moment,

During this stage,
Everything continues to play,
Forever in circular motion,

Going back to the start,
However how far,
In a song we call full circle,

Just ask any composer who knows,
Killing is love as,
Love is to be murdered,

Many,
Never notice,

Obvious to the observer,

People place themselves in,
Ques that,
Run around the world,

Seeing is believing,

Take a look at,
U,

Very ill,
With,
Xenophobic fever,

Yet the main attraction at the,
Zoo,

Moving On

Once a man went walking down,
A path paved with good intentions,
But hell was all he ever found,
And nowhere was where it led him,

His friends and family couldn't wait,
To remember to forget him,
And no one carried on his name,
For he had no wife or children,

When he passed none were sad,
Having no reason to forgive him,
And the news it read, "He's finally dead,
So let's get back to living",

Chapter Two

Where and When Inside My Mind I Go

Where and when inside my mind I go,
I go in desperation,
To vent out my frustration,
Over wasted words that take advantage,
Of an awful situation,

Where and when inside my mind I go,
I go for my protection,
Weary of detection,
To shield myself from twisted lies,
That take for granted my discretion,

Where and when inside my mind I go,
I go in indignation,
Seeking my salvation,
Away from clowns and middle men,
Out to steal my revelation,

Where and when inside my mind I go,
I go for relaxation,
On a personal vacation,
To a better place and time I find,
Is of my own creation,
Where and when inside my mind I go,

Live Forever

I could write about the flowers,
To fill up empty hours,

I could write about the seasons,
And all the things that never change,

I could write about the stars,
If I only had a reason,

And I could live forever,
If only in my dreams,

Wonder

Let it spill from me,
Like oil in the ocean,
White lies and corruption,
Drowning out my last emotion,

And let it flow from me,
Like a fire fueling our consumption,
As black as a coal miner,
In the lack of safety regulations,

Sell it out to me,
For a couple dollars cheaper,
Children tied to a table,
Eating from a dumpster,

Wait and you will see,
Nothing worth your veneration,
A 9/11 generation,
Crying why as we wonder,

War On The Border

The real war is on the border,
Said the man from Arizona,
Cops on every corner,
Looking out for fence jumpers,
Coyotes on the run,
Minute men on the hunt,
Guns provide the heat,
And angels bring the water,

So before you get deported,
Or searched without a warrant,
Keep your papers on your person,
When you head through Arizona,

The Great Escape

There's not enough ways to explain,
How life changes and stays just the same,

Like an endless uphill battle,

That will test you each step of the way,

And there's not enough words to describe,
The tricks that get played on the mind,

When everything seems better while looking back,
But was never as good at the time,

Proudly in you prime,

Before you joined the lines of those who wait,
To accept their fate and die,

Leaving all memory behind,
The kind of escape you cannot fake,
To drift away,
Goodbye,

Rebirth

Raping this Earth for all that it's worth,
Let it die and revive,
Then call it rebirth,

Like a lightning bolt in the night,
Striking right on the nerve,

Is it a sign from the sky,
Or a sign for the worst,

A sign of the times,
Our time to be heard,
The time of our lives,
And life is but short,

Netty

Again I curse for no reason,
But she drives me insane,
"Just the old bitch on the hill",
That's what she'll say,
On every new message,
It's always the same,
When she blows up my phone,
But can't remember my name,

Abstraction

Fade away into obscurity,
A world riddled with uncertainty,
Hidden by your enemies,
To cause you crisis of identity,

And welcome to absurdity,
A boredom littered by indignity,
An entity without intent,
Meant to test your sensibilities,

So forget about reality,
The frantic state of your mentality,
Equates to the duality,
Of what you know and feel,

Be real to individuality,
There's no originality,
Futile as fatality,
Finality is clear,

A Final Note

I'd shoot myself in the head,
If I wasn't already dead,
Let my mind bleed out on paper,
In a darker shade of red,

Chapter Three

Simplicity Pt. 1

This is my haiku,
I just wanted you to know,
You are on my mind,

Truth of Life

Life runs somewhere in between,
Our falsest hopes and wildest dreams,

Between burning hot and freezing cold,
This luke warm reality,
We've been sold,

Between the lines,
Behind the scenes,

The only truth to find,
Nothing as it seems,

Passive

Get used to making sacrifices,
And endless compromises,

Always in the midst of crisis,

Because high's the price we pay,

They'll hypnotize with their disguises,
Entice you with their vices,

Suffice with their devices,

To keep you passive through the day,

Ode

We will walk together,
Two byrds of a feather,
Hand in hand,
In the end,
Only freedom is forever,

Flying high and reaching far,
What are we searching for,

Something better to remember,

Or to be remembered for,

Aggressive

Prepare to be protective,
And overly possessive,

Go on the defensive,

Relentless and excessive,

Regressive and defective,
With no incentive to be saved,

Aggressive with the message,

To stay or go away,

Message

Sitting home alone,

I wrote a little rhyme,

For all the things we could have done,

If we only had the time,

Sitting by the phone,

Waiting for a sign,

Of anything that rings a bell,

Or strikes a cordless line,

Simplicity Pt. 2

Here I am again,
And no matter what I do,
You are on my mind,

Chapter Four

Introduction

Try to find the gumption,
To make a decent introduction,

Avoid any deception,
And meet you at every junction,

Try to leave a first impression,
Good enough to keep you guessing,

Do not be redundant,
Or reluctant with your message,

Try to leave them with a lesson,
At the end of every session,

Learn to function on assumptions,
With a new level of awareness,

Bargain

If there's nothing to be won,
Then what's the point in winning,

If there's no God to piss off,
Then what's the point in sinning,

When there's not a reason to believe,
Then what do you believe in,

Greed, wrath, envy, sloth,
Gluttony, pride, lust, or evil,

So live while you are living,
But give while you are getting,

The better end of any bargain,

In the end or the beginning,

Learning to Pretend

I apologize for all my lies,
And for what it's worth,

Was it worth it in the end,

To no surprise,
This thin disguise,

Has left me cold again,

Once I saw it in your eyes,
As high as hope,
An endless sky,

Kaleidoscope of new horizons,
Forever falling in,

But now your sight has faded,

The lights have all dimmed,

The life,
The drive,
The will inside,
All wilted in the wind,

But that's the grand design,
Something simply complicated,

Fated to be hated,

Still learning to pretend,

Photograph 07-09

Chapter One

Tunnel Vision

Circle Advice

Take all of your problems,
And paint your best face on 'em,
Wrap 'em all in pretty paper,
Then sell 'em out to the world,
Find a nice girl,
Who's will to solve 'em,
Take a load off yourself,
And split the burden with her,

Answer all of life's hard questions,
With a quick maybe,
Take another drink,
And then change the subject,
When in doubt,
Piss off the natives,
Make people pets,
And treat 'em like objects,

Remember everyone gets caught up,
In the circles they run in,
And if you haven't,
It's only a matter of time,
But don't fall in,
Again and again,
Unless all parties involved,
Are willing to call it a life,

So keep your options open,
If you're far from the end,
Remember that life is all circles,
With nowhere to finish,
And if your life seems over,
Find a new spot to begin,
Or piss on your home,
If that's where your heart is,

Long Train Southbound

Used to love the night life,
Yeah I used to ride the train,
Cruise to the end of the track,
And go right back again,
Yeah I used to look straight through the mirror,
Just to hide my sundried face,
Cough yourself up a little blood,
Yeah I used to love the taste,

Put on your Sunday suit,
Because the sky is caving in,
And I feel I might be heading,
Southbound again,

I woke the other morning,
And had thrown my life away,
The only reason that I could find,
Is that I didn't want one to stay,
But my thoughts seemed so much clearer,
And I found some words to say,
I also came upon the will to run,
At a faster pace,

No better time than now,
While my disguise is wearing thin,
Our rising sun is setting,
As I board the train again,

The long train southbound,

Shadow of the Pagan

It took only vice for advice,
To kill my only friend,
To let him know experience is to snake,
As apple is to wisdom,
He took an entire life he had,
And drove into the wilderness,
To find there is a hell,
We lie here through the seasons,
And how the wicked were all punished,
By time and loss of meaning,
For disobeying God,
And venturing further into Eden,
So he became his own God,
With no place for him in heaven,
To celebrate the light,
On any day that he'd been given,
And with the setting of the sun,
Fell the shadow of the pagan,
A story all but done,
A story barely written,
So as I drink the devil's blood,
Through the mirror it's him I'm seeing,
My only friend is gone,
My only friend was me,

Rat Race

The truth will always be,
Whichever version you determine,
Just another piper leading vermin,
Who find stability in change,
Creating rhythm so familiar,
Like walking in and on the water,
And although your part is over,
Still the song remains the same,

Burnt

Like reaching the end of a circle,
Or dividing yourself by one,
Alone we drift through skies of purple,
Falling further from the sun,
Always dreaming without sleeping,
And hiding where we're known,
Finding on the road,
That all signs lead back to home,
So tell me how am I to tell you,
That this time you had is gone,
Because I saw my old friend death again,
But here we're still rolling on,
On the burnt end of this candle,

Little Things

The little things they take,
Are the little things she keeps,
In a lonely house of cats,
That never seems to sleep,
Her island you can't drive on,
Animals crowd the streets,
And in this world you can't depend on,
She's as natural as a thief,

But she's aware of all her faults,
As well as everything else we do,
And in her life she plays her part,
So as not to get confused,
She's a riddle of a figure,
Sometimes simply too complex,
When she's locked up in her box,
With all the little things she's kept,

Empty Skies

Sitting here again,
And I know it won't be long,
Because the sky's been split in half,
And the love I had is gone,
Beat 'till I've been broken,
Bled 'till I've been drained,
All that's left for me to be,
Is by myself but not the same,

A lonely shadow of a figure,
Who liked his shell a little better,
Always waited out the weather,
Never saw the sun,
Forever empty skies,
Forever we are riding,
Forever and forever,
Forever ride alone,

Shades of Sin

As the sin in my soul lay rot,
Oh yes I believe in degrees of evil,
And in the shell of what we are,
The depths of some to none are equal,
It's what I fear the most,
To look over my shoulder and see their faces,
Openly exposed,
The lives I've ruined like wines I've tasted,

And I still have much time,
To open the doors of my mind with the keys that I've stolen,
Because we are all holding on to find,
If the palace of wisdom lies on the path we are roaming,
Lost in shades of sin,
And when it comes to excess there's always farther to go,
But with death constantly closing in,
Will forever I lie in this field of seeds that I've sewn?

Serial Monogamy

In the midst of a bitter winter heat,
I met a secret side of me kept separate,
A lying dog which desperate sleeps,
In a tiny bed that bleeds infection,
Under the advice of an old friend,
So far long withdrawn and disconnected,
A new way to spend a hard week's end,
Just back and forth with no direction,

Defining Time

In cohesive incoherent madness,
I inspire eyes,
To raise the sands,

Pulled apart,
To push again,
Defining time of who I am,

Never much left for speculation,
Nor a word of what you see,

Breathing out our best intentions,
Still inner tension's testing me,

Downtown Cigarette Pt. 1

In a miniature version of a larger city,
A place where we ride downtown,
And use for an ashtray,
Same old story on a slightly smaller scale,
Ignorant apes taking pride in a place,
That they constantly shit on,

From a young age around here,
There's so much you're exposed to,
As the savages ravage,
Where the children once played,
When parents get older but never grow up,
How can you leave to your children,
A world you refuse to create,

So in this miniature version of a much larger problem,
We listen to the stories of others who've wondered,
Why we stay in a place that offers us nothing,
Except more question than answers,
And a spot to toss butts on,

Downner

Can't escape a feeling,
Forever trotting through the bottom,
And this horse that I've been beating,
Guess I'll have to beat it even harder,
I've no logic left to offer,
Seems to be I'm strung,
Out on inside knowledge,
Now that my ride that died is gone,

The thought has reached the surface,
Supplant this life for peaceful nothing,
And although it seems absurd,
You could say it's in my blood,
I've seen it far too often,
And know well the repercussions,
Still I'd rather frustrate fate,
Than stay in the bottom of this world,

Peak

I found out today,
I'm just another slave to my past,
Those same memories that haunt me,
Are the ones I refuse to let go,
So can I move on,
And let yesterday mean nothing,
Or will I just die in this garden,
Where nothing can grow,

They say all of our lives,
We are constantly climbing,
Reaching for some peak,
But mine's a plateau,
Yeah believe it or not,
I've already been where you're going,
Where there's not much to see,
And far less to know,

Hurdles

Sometimes I'd rather be naïve,
This way of life's distracting me,
With all I'm too impatient to absorb,
Lines are met where lines are drawn,
Some might say our course is short,
Still no one knows how long we'll run,
Can we take our home again,
When what I've is mine,
And you've is yours,
It all depends on what's at stake,
Time that's wasted,
Time that's gone,
Seems a life is what it takes,
But if that's the game,
Then what is won,

New Light

For better or worse,
Things change here,

And that's just not the case back home,

Where you sit on your ass,
And wait for the master,
To remember to throw you a bone,

Well I can wait no more,
For you to turn my wheels,
Because this journey that I'm on,
I have to know it's real,
So when I close my eyes at night I know,
That my world still moves without me,
And when I wake in the morning to go,
I can feel new light around me,

It's then I am reborn,

Omelet

Wore out words cannot describe,
This whore of a world,
So tell me why even try to relate,

I give my love to dog and girl,
And the rest of you fucks can handle my hate,

Or die it makes no difference,
For you're already dead in this place,

While you sleep I dream in layers,
But I am still awake,

Starting aboriginal fires,
The only way left to create,

Making my omelet by cracking some eggs,
What a hell of an ending,
How does it taste?

Chapter Two

Insight

Epitaph

To whatever omnipotent force exists,
Whether present be or by Thy design,
To you confess my burdens,
Lay to rest,
Lest I end up out of favor,

Crust

Secure in insecurity,
As certain as uncertainty,
Despite whatever you might be thinking,
You think about your life,

Conjure up your demons,
While freedom feeds delusions,
Illusions from the dreaming,
A dream that is your life,

Sleeping through the sorrows,
Of tomorrows that you borrow,
Hollow head in gallows,
Folly throughout life,

So come take a plate of what their serving,
Both something fed and starving,
Just as bored as it is boring,
Your own tiny slice of life,

Dogs

I believe as breed we're borne feeble,
Like mutts on the street growing weaker,
When to rise above the rank of dog,
Is no longer enough of a reason,

New chains for every collar,
Treats for tricks throughout our seasons,
Rolling over for our masters,
In graves of garbage we've been digging,

Crack House

Drugs are the slice of heaven,
In this hell that I call home,
The only refuge to escape,
The only peace that I have known,

Instant pleasure to my senses,
In the midst of all this pain,
The least of my expenses,
Shelter from the rain,

Always reaching to the point,
In the end I'm only stoned,
So steadily I'm slipping,
Through the cracks that fill my home,

Public Service Announcement

Ramble warning words I say,
Confederate forces conspire succession,
Insurrection from a Southern way,
Dividing ties buy blue blood to ration,

As charming as the devil,
Our serpent speaks in tongues,
An orator on your level,
Casting broad into your homes,

With a larger plan to stall you out,

Stream of Consciousness

Live for today,
But remember today determines the way,
We remember yesterday tomorrow,

Hate can take a toll,
And when it's saved only drawing interest,
The longer that you hold,

Our love we carve in stone,
Freed by the keeper,
In this binding of souls,

The only thing immortal,
Not a surprise,
But I thought it best you should know,

Gateway

Brother, Brother, Brother,
Apollo none the other,
Become, Become, Become,
One with God and sun,

Sister, Sister, Sister,
Hold the Venus vissour,
The key to being stoned,
Let love light arch into your home,

And together we'll create a gate to the heavens,
That mortals seldom know,

Birthday Song

The baby's crying,
The whore is moaning,
My head is hurting,

The food is cold,
So's the weather,
And I'm too tired for learning,

I've come to know the wine,

It fills the urge to kill the surge,
Of wasted time of mind,

This wasted life of mine,

Behind a wall somewhere at home,

The food is cold,
And so's the weather,

You know I've never been this old,

I can feel it in my bones,

Every day is caked in gray,
Like tainted presents that I hold,

I wish again that I was young,

As I sit alone at my own table,
And watch my candle slowly burn,

But the day is almost gone,

Lay to rest like all the best,
Our party's waiting in the sun,

Walk

In between the hills,
In a valley I call home,
Alone I see my Grandpa,
Hand in hand with strangers that I've known,

And I will walk beside them,
In this valley that's my home,
To keep my love light shining,
All this love that I have known,

Demons are your friends,
Never let yourself be blinded,
The hard facts in the end,
See them in a silver lining,

Because the gold is only wanting,
And time is only binding,
Love is always waiting,
For those who seek to find it,

But you got to give in order to get,
And stay open to letting it have been,
Or you'll just end on the outside,
Stuck looking in,

Downtown Cigarette Pt. 2

Huddle together for heat,
Because it's cold out on the street,
Part of the painted crowd that gathers around,
A downtown cigarette,

Not a bird of a leaf in a tree,
Wearing only a patch for a sleeve,
I met a man who burned his hand,
On a downtown cigarette,

Poetic License

Part of the poets' practice,
To pluck your heart strings,
While he picks your pockets,

Part of the prisons' problem,
Preaching peace,
To plunder prophets,

The poetic license to steal,
Something to which we're all entitled,
Unbridled as the will,
Part of the present party though uninvited,

Tetherless Tethered

A man makes his own way,
If ever could he ever,
Or so I've heard them say,
Either way it sounded pretty clever,

But then again it's in the wind,
Will we ever know never,
To find out in the end,
You can't out weather the weather,

And so it all began,
The story of the tetherless tethered,
Who the farther that he swam,
Could never get deeper,

The only dreamer in a world,
Filled with too many sleepers,
Oyster spit or pearls,
You decide your own reason,

For being a being just being yourself,
Trading treasure for shell,
Off of the shelf,
And out on the illness which kills us too well,

Freedom Song

Hot on the tracks of a train called life,
Moving fast down the highway,

Out of luck,
The rain is pouring,
With the wind blowing my way,

Wear a scar on my right arm,
To recall freedom while imprisoned,

True story of a man and his guitar,
And the hand that he's been dealing,

Got a kid and woman in the city,
But my gun's out on the highway,

Got the trigger always ready,
War boots in the bars,
Crashing cars and getting sideways,

Time's on my side,
Though I've left the worst of them behind me,
Friends and family,
Giving love and finding God to guide me,
Free in every sense,
This same hat I've worn for years,

Because in the woods it's wild,
And the best are playing here,

Singing songs of America,

Fort Hood 11/14/09

The counselor gone mad,
A Columbine in Texas,
The start of something worse,
If we do not learn the lesson,

Twelve already dead,
Thirty counting blessings,
New massacres are fed,
By so-called martyrs of the present,

False stirrings of rebellion,
That I pray to God aren't spreading,
Because there is no reward in heaven,
For this kind of senseless killing,

So go ahead and mark my words,
This is only the beginning,
Of something so much worse,
We can only start to fathom,

Divorcing Nature

She came and left me in a storm,
And put me on the road,

Raining down like fire,
And breathing down me hard,

Thought I'd wait it out,
But the levee's over flown,

'Cause Katrina the old lady,
She done took my home,

My car was swept away,
In the wake of our divorce,

In the end we went our separate ways,
And nature ran its' course,

The flood had hit the gates,
And now I'm glad she's gone,

'Cause Katrina the old lady,
She done took my home,

Spasm

Victim to a spasm,
Another stroke of genius,
This heart attack I'm having,
You know I'm only slowly bleeding,
Stop the flow into my brain,
I'm choking can't you see it,
Maybe I'm insane,
But you have to be it to be it,

Feeding off the fat,
Bad cholesterol I'm eating,
Breathing giving back,
What the catheter ain't reading,
Building up a plaque,
Didn't stress an ego,
Still the nurse's aid must graduate,
Before she can be my surgeon,

Chapter Three

Open Scope

An Act of Wedding

Waking up to bells and rings,
The buzz of bees and birds of song,
Usher in altered spring,
This winter's lasted far too long,

The Great Social Contract

Either I can see,
Or I'm used to being blind,
But for better or worse,
Is the man's only clause,

Dogs of different breeds,
Being as we are,
Of course she's bound to curse,
And put our noses to the floor,

Ladies take it faithfully,
It rightfully is yours,
He'll be ok to play with other dogs,
As long as you cut your leashes short,

Style Idols

Style idled,
The new idol style,
But it fits you like it should,

Who else on this Earth but you,
Could make going nowhere,
Look so good,

Bossman The Clown

While you might join the sideshow,
Still I must run the circus,
New freaks for every week,
With purpose of peaking people's interest,

Speaking directly to the public,
With perfect poetic diction,
Driving life up to the stage,
While drowning down in deep dissention,

So spare me by your sarcasm,
You better never ever not let it,
Because you're talking to Bossman the Clown,
And don't you ever forget it,

The Battle of Rap

Stand at the gates,
Of the enemy hate,
Throw down your arms,
Begin bearing the blame,
Of shame you've brought home,
For being bought out in the game,
Gaily singing your songs,
While simultaneously selling your name,

Ok to the point,
But there is such a thing,
Of too much of the same,
So don't be afraid,
To remix what you match,
That's how you're supposed to create,

Or so I've been told,
At least that's what they say,
Either you're out in the cold,
Or you live in the flame,
Battling platinum plaques of fame,

Old School

Rich kids fake field trips,
To the poor school,

Permission slips,
On printed paper,
While pinching signatures from fools,

As younger teachers fill the bleachers,

Standing out in older schools,

Pencil Dick Freud

Proud to hold a pencil dick,
Of average length,
When stiff as wood,

But will it ever measure up,
And erase this page,
Of gray I've drawn,

Plotted out in black and white,
But printed on a line of blue,
Send it in an envelope,
And male it back to you,

I can't collar myself yellow,
If the world tints a different hue,
Graph it out in groups of gray,
Straight from me to you,

And if a cigarette is what needs lit,
Then put your lips on this,
And if you don't enjoy the taste,
I'm sad you missed the oral fix,

Proctology

If ever you'd want to know more,
Try to take a deeper look,
Drag your sorry ass to the store,
And buy my next book,

Or end up as empty as my wallet,
Will it ever be full,
From this prophetic poop,
I've been scooping from you,

Taking tricks of the trade,
And putting to use,
Forcing technical tools,
In the most private of places,

A proctologist's job,
Come on people let's face it,
To the rear we are near,
Picking on cancer,

Conception

Getting off inside your head,
Guess there's nowhere else for me to go,
Got to grab attention bad,
Going back to gardens sewn,

Transcending expectations,
Taking trips to different points of view,
Tackle waves on this vacation,
Tumble through this ocean blue,

T-Ball

First you must step up to the plate,
With two sticks and one ball,
Then try to run around the diamond,
To get back to home,
All without being struck out,
Or tagged by the glove,
There's no I in this team,
Or in this game we call love,

Chapter Four

Reflecting Light

History Repeated

Constantly in a war with ourselves,
That's anything but civil,
Worn weary from the worthless wage,
Of wasted towns we level,

Emancipate on paper,
Still your slaves are bounded,
The struggle isn't over,
For those whose freedom is unfounded,

Heartless Artist

Carving out a sculpture,
From a lonely heart of stone,
As rough as it is rugged,
With a beauty all its own,

This medium I've chosen,
To make my way back home,
And if you never get it,
Then I guess you'll never know,

Painting pretty pictures,
Out of ugly undertones,
An artist and a camera,
See the world upside down,

Lifted through the lenses,
Let the image take its form,
In strokes put on a pallet,
Placed on a petty stool,

Breathe

Remember to breathe,
When put to the test,

A personal mantra,
That I've adopted,

And it hasn't failed me yet,
This I swear by codes of liars,

Put the tick tock of the clock,
On the wall behind you,

Nor friend or foe,
Just time to blind you,

Remember to breathe,
I keep repeating,
Then you'll find,
They cannot stump you,

Hope

Holding a key to my heart,
You've opened the door,
Broke through the lock,
Helped me rise from the floor,

Cleaned up my mess,
Spared me the smoke,
Which has started this fire,
That now heats our home,

I love you the best,
That isn't a joke,
And I'm only blessed,
To have you as my hope,

To Ashley

Rabid Rabbit

Look to the stars,
With long ears,
And worn fur,

Live in the wild,
When not searching for food,

Run from the rest,
But when protecting your nest,
Fester in rage,
And give it your all,

Chapter Five

Click

A Conductor of One

If I am to be an instrument,
I pray I stay in tune,
My Musician makes mad melody,
My medley maestro muse,

In conquest of composition,
Carry chords through narrow channels,
Call out on a little phone,
With no one at home to answer,